Flying

Conquer Your Fear of Flying

Captain Adrian Akers-Douglas

and Dr George Georgiou, Ph.D.

Cartoons by Matt Wilde

SUMMERSDALE

First published 1996
Second edition 1997
Third edition 2000

This edition copyright © Adrian Akers-Douglas and George Georgiou 2002

Images copyright © Matt Wilde 2002

Summersdale Publishers Ltd
46 West Street
Chichester
West Sussex
PO19 1RP
England

www.summersdale.com

ISBN 1 84024 245 0

The extract from *Taking the Fear out of Flying* (1990) by Dr Maurice Yaffé is reprinted by kind permission of David & Charles Publishers.

Printed in Denmark by Nørhaven Paperback A/S

About the Authors

Adrian Akers-Douglas began his flying career with the RAF and now flies Airbus A320 aircraft with Eurocypria Airlines. As well as flying ordinary passenger flights, he also trains and checks his colleagues in the aircraft and in simulators.

He has a wife and two daughters and makes his home in a Cypriot village.

His profits from this book are donated to the Cyprus Conservation Foundation.

He would very much welcome any comment or feedback on this book, and can be contacted by e-mail at: adrian@spidernet.com.cy

Dr George J. Georgiou, Ph.D. is a natural medicine practitioner, researcher and writer. He is the director of the Natural Therapy Centre, which specialises in aspects of natural medicine.

Dr Georgiou is married to a clinical psychologist with four children, and enjoys flying a private plane, horse riding, and living close to nature.

Matt Wilde lives in Cyprus and does his own thing.

Contents

Introduction

The writers hope that this book will help the many people who are apprehensive about flying. Sometimes unnecessary anxiety is caused by events which airline crews may take for granted, including aspects of flights that are mystifying and even alarming to less frequent flyers.

Part I of this book takes readers through a typical flight, explaining in non-technical terms just what is happening at any point in the journey. This is followed by Part II, which deals frankly with some of the aspects of flying which may be a cause of worry.

Part III offers a professional explanation of the phenomena that cause anxiety and offers an unusual perspective on dealing with it.

Two appendices offer further advice on dealing with fear of flying.

If this little publication helps readers to come to terms with an extremely safe form of travel, it will have fulfilled its function.

PART I

The Flight Now Departing . . .

In the beginning . . .

Centre of Attention

As you leave home to check in for your flight, the professionals who will be responsible for your comfort and safety will probably already be at work. You may have seen how an aircraft becomes the centre of a hive of activity when it lands. Baggage and catering is unloaded and loaded, fuel and water are pumped on, the cabin is cleaned and readied for the next flight, and a series of checks are performed.

Aircraft are usually serviced on a continuing basis. Whenever they land, certain checks and examinations will be undertaken. Then, at prearranged intervals, the aircraft is taken out of service for a few hours, days, or even weeks while ever more elaborate maintenance is carried out.

Whilst the engineers, caterers, cleaners, baggage handlers, and refuellers are attending to the aircraft, the flight-deck and cabin crews will be reporting for their briefings.

Planning

The flight-deck crew is supplied with all the details concerning the flight: the weather en route and at the destination; the number of passengers and the weight of freight being carried; a computer-generated plan of the route, predicting the flight time and fuel needed; and any other details which might affect the flight.

The captain then decides on the amount of fuel to be loaded, which will be enough to fly to the destination, then to another airfield should the destination, for any reason, be closed when the flight arrives, and an extra amount on top of that.

Simultaneously, a flight plan, giving details of the

time and height at which the aircraft will pass over various points along the route, together with its estimated time of arrival at the destination, is sent to all the air traffic control centres responsible for regulating the flow of traffic along the route which the flight will take. These centres then start to integrate our flight with all the other flights with which we shall be sharing airspace.

Eventually, we will be given a time at which our flight must depart in order to fit in with the other traffic. Usually, this is very close to the scheduled departure time.

Whilst the flight-deck crew complete their briefing, the cabin crew leader will be ensuring that his or her colleagues are fully aware of what they have to do in any emergency, that they know where all the related equipment is to be found on the aircraft, and how to operate it. Only then will they turn to how they intend to conduct the passenger service, the needs of any special cases (handicapped people, unaccompanied children, etc) who will be on board, and any specific details relating to the flight.

The cabin crew will discuss the needs of unaccompanied children

At least half an hour before the flight is due to depart, the crew will go out to the aircraft. The cabin crew check the emergency equipment, such as fire extinguishers, medical kits, and the portable oxygen bottles which are kept in the cabin (for use if a passenger is taken ill), and then they ensure that all the catering and bars are in order. They will also ensure that the cabin looks neat and tidy for our 'guests'.

Checking the Aircraft

Meanwhile, the pilots will be running through an exhaustive series of checks on the various aircraft systems, and loading the day's flight information into the computers. One of the pilots will also examine the outside of the aircraft, double-checking an inspection that has already been carried out by the ground engineers.

When the crew is satisfied with the condition of the aircraft, the passengers will be called. By the time the 'customers' arrive, much of the activity around the aircraft will have subsided, although there will probably still be last minute baggage and freight to load, and you may see the flight-deck crew still busy with their checks.

When everyone is on board, the cabin crew count heads. It is important that exactly the number of passengers expected are actually on board. Too many, and someone has probably got on the wrong flight. Too few, and a baggage identification procedure has to be implemented to ensure that no one has checked in any luggage and then 'disappeared'. In these days of random terrorism, such risks are unacceptable.

Some people have cottoned on to the fact that if their bags are on board, it is unlikely that they will be left behind, and have abused the system by keeping everyone else waiting long after the aircraft doors should have been closed. This is extremely frustrating for both the crew and all the other passengers who have managed to get themselves to the aircraft on time, especially in these days of crowded skies, when we are given a place in the queue of aircraft waiting to start, with long delays the penalty for missing one's turn.

In the past, having to do a 'baggage ident' took a long time, and we were prepared to do almost anything to find the 'lost sheep' before having to resort to unloading and have the passengers point out their own belongings.

However, dear reader, be warned: if you have been playing this game, technology is catching up with you! More and more airlines and airports now have very sophisticated baggage tracking systems which will indicate almost exactly where in the aircraft's hold the miscreant's bag is. It is now very much easier to trace luggage and heave it off the aeroplane if you don't show up on time.

Doors Closed

If the passenger count is correct, we can get going. The last of the ground personnel leave, and the doors are closed.

You may then hear the cabin crew leader telling his staff to 'arm the doors'. Each of the doors and the overwing exits are equipped with slides to help people escape from the cabin in the event of an emergency landing. These slides are inflated by compressed air (sometimes they can also be used as life-rafts if the aircraft has to land on water). When the slides are 'armed', they will automatically inflate when the doors are opened.

There is little quite so embarrassing as forgetting to 'disarm' the slides after landing, arriving at the terminal, opening the door, and watching aghast as a writhing rubber slide unwinds in front of the bemused passengers and ground staff! Thus it is essential that the cabin crew check that the slides are disarmed after the aircraft has landed safely at its destination.

A writhing rubber slide unwinds

Starting Up

Clear to Start

The pilots will then call the control tower for permission to start engines. Providing all the air traffic control regions through which the aircraft will pass and the destination airport can accept the flight without delays, permission to start will be given.

If, on the other hand, the airspace along the route is congested, we may suffer one of those tedious delays awaiting a place in the queue. If this happens, and the delay is going to be lengthy, the captain will contact the airline's operations office to try to work out an alternative routing which may be less busy. This sometimes works, but at other times, especially at peak holiday periods, there is just such a volume of traffic that all routes are jammed. Then patience and good humour are the qualities most in demand from passengers and crew.

With permission to start granted, the flight really comes to life, accompanied by what may seem to some people like rather alarming whines, clunks, whirrs, and various other sounds.

Start Engines

The first noticeable indication that the engines are being started is when the flow of conditioned air to the cabin is cut off.

The engines on most aircraft are started using compressed air from the same source that supplies the air conditioning and electricity on the ground – a small jet engine (called an auxiliary power unit, or APU), usually located in the tail of the airliner. The APU cannot provide enough air for both air conditioning and the engine starter system, so the cabin conditioning is shut off for the short time it takes to get the engines going.

The aircraft often trembles slightly as the engines gather speed and the cabin lights may flicker briefly as the engine-driven generators take over the supply of electricity from the APU. Once the engines have started, you may hear a series of strange sounds, apparently coming from underneath the floor of the cabin. These are caused by the pilots moving the 'slats' and 'flaps' into the position required for take-off.

High Lift Devices

'Slats' and 'flaps' are the bits that droop down from the

front and back of the wing on take-off and landing. Flaps hang down at the back of the wing, and slats at the front. They are known as 'high lift devices'. What are they for?

Aircraft wings are a compromise which have to meet two different requirements. During the cruise at high altitude we want the aeroplane to fly quickly. This requires a certain shape of wing. But when we are taking off and landing, we want to fly slowly so that we do not use up too much runway. This requires a completely different shape of wing. Since no one has yet invented the fully flexible rubber wing, the designers arrange a compromise by fitting slats and flaps to the wing, which effectively alter its shape to fit the phase of flight.

The slats and flaps are electrically or hydraulically operated, which accounts for those sounds as they move in and out.

The flight-deck crew complete a series of checks after the engines are started, and then get permission from the control tower to taxi out to the runway.

Wheels Rolling

If you are sitting near a window, you may see the ground engineer, who has supervised the start-up, waving the crew off and perhaps holding up what appears to be a broad red ribbon. This is attached to a finger-sized pin, which is inserted into the nose-wheel assembly while the aircraft is pushed back from its parking stand. This pin disables the nose-wheel steering system, so that the tractor which pushes the aircraft back does not damage the aeroplane's steering mechanism. The crew want to know for sure that the ground engineer has pulled this pin out and thus restored their ability to steer the aircraft on the ground, which is why he waves the red ribbon at them.

The ground engineer waves the aircraft off

As the aircraft taxies out, you may see various panels rising and falling on the wing as the pilots check the controls. As they proceed towards the runway, the crew will also be receiving their instructions for the departure and the route to be followed for the flight from the control tower. Whilst all this is going on, the cabin crew will be showing the passengers what to do if an emergency should occur during the flight: the aviation equivalent of the traditional nautical 'boat drill'.

Safety Drills

It really is worth paying attention to these demonstrations. In the extremely unlikely event of something happening during the flight, there may not be time to repeat all this briefing. How many of those people with their heads buried in newspapers during the demonstration before take-off will know where to find the emergency exits or how to put on their oxygen masks? Apart from anything else, it's pretty soul-destroying for the cabin crew to be performing in front of a completely uninterested audience!

Eventually, everything is ready in the cockpit, the cabin, and with the air traffic control authorities. The flight is cleared for take-off. For the pilots, this and the landing are the two best moments in the whole flight. Those who are apprehensive about flying may not share our enthusiasm for the experience, which is always exhilarating, no matter how often we have done it.

Take-off

Take-off and landing are the two most critical phases of the flight, simply because these are the times when the aircraft is closest to the ground. Aeroplanes and terra firma do not mix well. It is extremely rare for disaster to befall an aircraft high in the sky – it is when it meets the ground in unscheduled fashion that catastrophe ensues. On take-off, the aircraft must accelerate from rest to a speed at which it will fly – typically about 160 mph in a jet – in a bit over a mile.

Engine Power

On the most modern aircraft, the engine thrust is set automatically. A computer linked to the throttles calculates the exact power needed for take-off, which is usually less than the engines' maximum capabilities. In just the same way that it is not good practice to put the accelerator in a car 'flat to the floor', so the pilots can reduce the wear and tear on their engines by only using as much power as is actually required, taking into account the prevailing conditions (the weight of the aircraft and the wind and temperature at the airfield).

The maximum thrust available from modern jet engines is awesome: a large engine like a Rolls Royce RB211 produces a power output equivalent to that of about 46 family cars.

In the passenger cabin, the start of the take-off is marked by a rising whine from the engines, a distinct push in the back due to the formidable rate of acceleration, and sometimes a rumble or series of thumps from the wheels as they pass over the lights embedded into the runway.

What If ... ?

As the aircraft races down the runway, the crew will be monitoring the instruments for the slightest sign of a malfunction, and will be checking that the aircraft is accelerating normally.

People often ask: 'What happens if an engine fails during the take-off?' The answer is: 'Nothing terribly dramatic.' The fact is that the pilots are *expecting* an engine to fail at the most critical point of the take-off! If this sounds like just the sort of titbit to put you off flying forever, let's explain a bit of the philosophy which lies behind all aircraft design and flying training.

Very elaborate (and very expensive) efforts are made to ensure that nothing goes wrong with an aircraft, or, if it does, that the crew are capable of dealing with virtually any situation that confronts them.

Safety First

Thus, on an aeroplane, any system of importance is duplicated, triplicated, or even quadruplicated. If one should fail, there is another to take over. Typically, a twin-engined aircraft will have three generators to provide the necessary electricity, any one of which would be sufficient for the aeroplane's needs. If the whole lot quit, there are powerful batteries in reserve. The controls are worked by hydraulic power from three separate systems, and again any one of these would be enough. If they all give up, there is a fourth emergency system which would ensure that the aircraft could be flown to a safe landing, and so on. Very much a 'belt and braces' concept.

The Right Stuff?

But ultimately the safety of each flight lies in the hands

of the crew, no matter how sophisticated the aeroplane may be. Airlines spend very large sums of money training their crews to extremely high standards; indeed, aircrew are probably one of the few professions in the world in which the individual's proficiency is constantly being reviewed.

A pilot typically undergoes at least seven medical or flight checks each year, during which he or she will be required to demonstrate a high degree of skill, knowledge, fitness, and resourcefulness. And to ensure that there are no 'cosy arrangements' whereby colleagues within an airline set lenient standards for each other, the airlines themselves are independently supervised by government civil aviation inspectors, who periodically sit in on these examinations to ensure that a high standard is maintained.

The crews are expected to be able to cope with anything that happens. Thus, we always assume the worst – for example that an engine *will* fail on take-off, and that it will choose the worst possible moment to do so.

Thus the aircraft's weight is limited so that the take-off could be continued safely (after a certain speed is reached) even if an engine does buck tradition and fail.

Actually, engines very rarely do fail, especially at the most critical point in the take-off. (Except in the training simulator, when everything goes wrong almost all the time.)

All Systems 'Go'

Anyway, back to the take-off. The pilot flying the aircraft will be handling the controls (there is no such thing yet as an 'automatic' take-off), whilst the other pilot scans the instruments and calls out certain speeds as they are reached.

The most important of these is called 'V1', or 'decision speed'. Below this speed, if anything goes wrong we abandon the take-off and stop. Above this speed, we are going too fast to bring the aircraft to a halt on the remaining length of runway, so it is safer to continue with the take-off, resolve the problem once we are airborne, and then decide whether to continue with the flight or return to land. Even if an engine fails at V1, the take-off can be continued perfectly safely, a manoeuvre we regularly practise in the flight simulator.

The next speed the crew are looking for is the 'rotation speed'. This is the speed at which the aircraft can be lifted off the runway. It is called rotation speed because this is literally what the pilot handling the controls does: he eases back the control column, the nose of the aircraft rises, and within moments we are airborne and climbing away from the runway.

Up, Up, and Away

In modern aircraft, the angle of climb can appear very steep. In fact, the actual angle will be a bit less than 20 degrees, but it can feel like much more as you are tilted back in your seat.

As soon as the pilots are certain that the aircraft is clear of the ground and is climbing normally, they raise the wheels. This often leads to a series of whines and thumps as the hydraulic system opens and closes the undercarriage doors, and heaves the heavy wheel assemblies into their cavities.

A minute or so later, more sounds may announce that the time has come to retract the slats and flaps. If you are sitting near the wing, you can see these surfaces sliding into position.

The aircraft will now be accelerating and climbing fast, but in a busy control zone such as those around major airports, the crew are often instructed by air traffic control to interrupt the climb to allow other departing or arriving aircraft to pass above them. This can sometimes cause changes in engine noise or aircraft attitude as the pilots level off, reduce engine power (so as not to go too fast), and then increase the power and pull up into a climb again when they are cleared to do so.

The aircraft will soon be away from the busy area around the airport, and then the climb is usually a smooth and steady ascent to the cruising altitude. This will take about 20 or 30 minutes.

When the aircraft levels off you may hear the engine note change as power is reduced to that needed for level flight. Later on during the trip, as fuel is burned off and the aircraft becomes lighter, the crew may climb again, because generally speaking jet aircraft perform best when flying as high as their weight allows.

The maximum height at which a jet airliner can fly varies from type to type, but is usually around 41,000 to 43,000 feet. Concorde trundles along at about 60,000 feet, an appropriately rarefied altitude from which to look down on the peasants below.

The Cruise

The cruising part of the flight, which may last from just a few minutes to interminable hours on a long journey, is generally pretty boring for the passengers.

The imagination of the apprehensive passenger runs riot

The lack of stimulation often allows the imagination of the apprehensive passenger to run riot. Perhaps the crew have died of food-poisoning? Wild-eyed hijackers have secretly taken over?

Happily, these things only occur in disaster movies. What is actually happening up front is much less dramatic. The autopilot will be flying the aircraft, probably coupled to an automatic navigation system. One pilot will be monitoring this and keeping watch for other aeroplanes, whilst the other handles the radio communications with air traffic control, checks the fuel consumption, and obtains the weather reports for various en route airfields in case a diversion is needed. (Passengers occasionally have heart attacks or some other medical problem and require urgent hospitalisation. We therefore keep tabs on the conditions at airports as we pass them.)

Autopilot

Usually the autopilot is used extensively on each flight. On modern aeroplanes, the automatic pilot (never, incidentally, called 'George' except by people whose aviation lore began and ended with Biggles) can be engaged about four seconds after take-off, and does not have to be disconnected until after the aircraft has landed. In between, the autopilot – if it is connected to a navigation computer – will fly the aircraft along the pre-selected route without the need for any further assistance from the crew. That said, most pilots spend at least some of the time flying the aircraft manually – simply because it is such fun!

The high point for the crew during this time is when a stewardess produces the meal trays. (Yes – we do eat different meals. And the other pilot always gets the better one.)

The other pilot always gets the better meal

Engine Noise

During cruising flight you may detect the engine noise varying slightly. The engine power is controlled by a computer which is constantly calculating the most economical speed at which to fly. This speed varies slightly in response to the wind, the temperature of the atmosphere, and the weight of the aircraft (which decreases as fuel is used up). Thus the computer from time to time commands small alterations of engine thrust, and these changes are sometimes audible in the passenger cabin. They are absolutely routine, but are apparently a source of concern to some people.

Other Aircraft – Fellow Travellers

Others worry if they spot another aircraft out of the window. There is no reason why you shouldn't see other aeroplanes: they have every right to be there! However, we pass each other so quickly that, seen sideways on from the passenger cabin, they are usually in sight for only a few seconds, and thus missed unless you happen to be glancing out at just the right time.

The vertical separation between aeroplanes is always at least a thousand feet. However, a jumbo jet passing a thousand feet above you looks very impressive: the sight is known in aviation circles as 'aluminium overcast'.

Knowing Where We're Going

The world is covered by a network of 'airways', rather like corridors in the sky, along which aircraft fly under the watchful eye of air traffic control. These airways are usually about ten miles wide, and many thousands of feet 'thick'. They run between radio beacons on the ground, which the flight crews use for navigation.

If the flight is over an area with few or no radio beacons (such as deserts or oceans), modern aircraft are equipped with extremely accurate self-contained navigation systems which use either laser gyros or satellite signals (GPS – global positioning system), or both. We no longer have to sit in the cockpit running our fingers along a grubby map, or following a ploughed furrow across the desert, as our predecessors did in the old, audacious days.

Within the airways, flights are separated both vertically and horizontally. If the aircraft is being monitored by an air traffic control radar, no other aeroplane is allowed to approach closer than 20 miles if the two flights are at the same height, and within 1000 feet if they are passing one above the other. If no radar is available (for example over oceans or deserts), then the horizontal separation is about 80 miles – roughly ten minutes' flying time. Thus, each aircraft flies within a large, protected 'bubble' of private airspace.

Air Traffic Control

Air traffic control tells each flight the route it is to take and the height at which to fly, occasionally ordering the pilots to change altitude if the desired separation from other aircraft cannot be maintained. The pilots are in constant radio contact with the controllers, and are passed from one regional centre to another as the flight progresses. English is used as the standard language of communication everywhere in the world. So although pilots always maintain a good lookout, the main responsibility for keeping aircraft out of each other's way rests with the air traffic controllers.

Contrary to what is often thought, an airliner's radar is not designed to pick up other aircraft. It is there primarily to detect bad weather, and enable the crew to avoid thunderstorms and turbulent cloud. The aircraft's radar can also map the ground to a limited extent, and so is sometimes used as a navigational aid.

Modern aircraft are equipped with a device called Traffic Alert and Collision Avoidance System (always known by its acronym, TCAS), which detects other aircraft providing that they also carry similar equipment. In this case, computers on board each aircraft exchange information concerning their respective flight paths. If there is a potential conflict, the systems let the pilots know of the problem by alerting them to the presence of the other flight, displaying the 'intruder' on our navigation screen.

If the situation continues to worsen, the TCAS becomes ever more agitated, changing the appearance of the symbol on the navigation display and finally 'speaking' to the pilots, giving orders such as 'climb!' or 'descend!' if a real possibility of collision develops.

The TCAS system is clever: the computers aboard the aircraft decide between themselves which aircraft should climb and which should descend, so that they don't both take evasive action in the same direction.

Even without TCAS, the present air traffic arrangements work very well, and the incidence of near misses is extremely low (although they are usually blown out of all proportion in the popular press on the rare occasions when they do occur). Given, then, that we are all flying along these airways, it is not surprising that you will occasionally see another aeroplane passing by.

Phenomena

At night, we sometimes amuse ourselves on the flight deck by flashing our lights in greeting to other voyagers in the dark skies, a harmless diversion that has probably given rise to untold reports of 'flying saucers' by observant citizens on the ground, thousands of feet below us.

The white vapour trails which you can sometimes see etched against a blue sky as an airliner flies high overhead are not composed of smoke from the engines, as is sometimes thought. These trails are caused by the hot gasses from the engines' exhausts mixing with the cold atmosphere. (Typically it is about 57 degrees Celsius below zero at the heights at which airliners cruise.) Under certain conditions of temperature and humidity, the gasses condense to form 'clouds', the trails which you can see.

Who's Calling?

Meanwhile, back in the passenger cabin, what has the apprehensive flyer found to worry about? What about those electronic 'ding-dongs' that send a stewardess scurrying towards the flight deck or cause her to mutter into a telephone?

Most modern airliners are equipped with a series of electronic chimes, specially devised to madden the passenger who is attempting to doze off. The chimes are of different tones and each has a meaning.

One chime means that the flight-deck crew are calling – almost always that is just for another cup of coffee, but the cabin crew respond immediately in case the pilots want to pass a message of operational significance. (In a real emergency, most airlines use a pre-arranged coded phrase from the captain over the public address system to alert the cabin crew.)

Another tone means that a passenger has pressed the call button on his seat or in the panel above his head. Another, that one of the cabin crew in one part of the aircraft wants to speak to another crew member somewhere else.

There is even a tone which means that someone is stuck in one of the toilets and needs help.

Getting There

As the flight approaches its destination the crew will often switch on the 'fasten seat belts' sign as they begin the descent, not necessarily because they are expecting any turbulence on the way down, but more to give the cabin crew time to clear up before the landing, an almost impossible task if people are still milling about in the aisles.

The descent will be marked by a gentle lowering of the aircraft's nose, and the sound of the engine power being reduced. You will also feel your ears beginning to 'pop' as the pressurisation system starts to reduce the altitude in the cabin.

Going Down

Throughout the flight, the cabin is pressurised and air conditioned by air from the engines. So whilst the aeroplane itself is cruising at perhaps 35,000 feet, the altitude in the cabin never goes above about 8,000 – roughly the same height as an Alpine ski resort. However, most airports are much lower than this, so during the descent the pressurisation system gently brings the cabin down to the same height as the airport. Although the aeroplane may be descending much faster, the cabin in which you are sitting will effectively be coming down at around 400 feet per minute, about the same rate as a lift.

It is this reduction in cabin height which causes your ears to 'pop', as air pressure builds up inside them. Most people have no trouble coping with this: yawning, moving your jaws, holding your nose and gently blowing are all effective ways of clearing the ears. The writer has also been told that Sudafed tablets are useful. (Ear plugs, incidentally, are useless.) If you have an infant with you, let him or her howl on the way down: a highly efficient way of clearing the ears not readily available to adults.

Problems sometimes occur if people are suffering from heavy colds or sinus infections. In these cases, air trapped in the inner ear passages can cause discomfort or even pain. In extreme cases, it can even lead to a burst eardrum. Therefore, if you have a heavy cold or sinus trouble, it may be wise to ask a doctor's advice before you fly.

As the aircraft approaches the airport, it will start to slow down. Once again you may hear noises as the crew operate the slats and flaps on the wings, and as the undercarriage is lowered. The engine sound may also be varying quite noticeably as the pilots change speed and compensate for the extra drag on the aeroplane caused by the extended landing-gear and flaps.

Blind Landing

At this stage, the pilots are probably being directed by a radar controller towards two narrow electronic beams which are being projected from transmitters close to the runway. One of these beams is aligned with the centre line of the runway. The other is projected upwards at a shallow angle from the threshold of the runway: it defines the correct glide path to the runway.

These two beams are collectively known as an Instrument Landing System (ILS, for short).

The ILS can be picked up by instruments in the cockpit. All the pilots have to do is to follow these beams; they then know that the aircraft is properly aligned with the exact centre of the runway, and is coming down on a slope which will bring it over the threshold of the runway at just the right height to make a landing. This can be done either by the pilots flying the aircraft manually and following their instruments, or automatically by the aeroplane's autopilot. And of course, this can all take place in cloud, mist or fog – the runway itself may not be visible until the very last moments before touchdown.

Most modern aircraft are equipped with automatic landing systems, which means that the aeroplane can carry out the landing in conditions – such as thick fog – in which a human being would be unable to do so. 'Autoland', as it is called, has been around for many years, and it has now reached such a degree of sophistication that the problem nowadays is not one of being able to land and stop on a fog-shrouded runway, it is simply that the pilot still has to be able to see enough to steer the airliner off the runway after landing and find his way to the airport terminal.

The pilot still has to steer the aircraft to the terminal building

For this reason, the minimum visibility in which even an automatic landing can take place is 75 metres.

The Landing Queue

People sometimes see what appears to be a constant stream of aeroplanes approaching one behind the other to land at a busy airport, and they wonder what happens if you encounter the slipstream of a preceding aircraft. This sometimes happens, especially on a calm day when there is no wind to help dissipate the aeroplane's wake. However, the air traffic controllers who are arranging the flow of traffic leave a gap of several miles between each aeroplane, the exact amount depending on the relative sizes of the two aircraft (if a small aircraft is following a large one, the separation must be greater). In practice this means that even if we do meet the wake of another aeroplane, it will only be felt as a slight shudder.

Touchdown

Pilots of civilian airliners aim to land about 300 metres along the runway from the threshold, so as to make quite certain that they do not inadvertently touch the ground before the beginning of the tarmac (grass on the wheels being difficult to explain to the chief pilot).

Grass on the wheels is difficult to explain to the chief pilot

Landings vary from 'greasers' (so soft you don't even know you're down) to mortifying 'pile-drivers': the latter are very rare, although we've all done them. A typical landing speed for a large jet is around 150 mph.

If you can see the wings, you may notice a series of small 'doors' pop open from the upper surface just after touchdown. These are called 'lift dumpers' and they do just that: they destroy the lift generated by the wing so that all the weight of the aircraft is placed firmly on the wheels to maximise the effect of braking. (If you notice these 'doors' lifting up in flight, it is because some aircraft use them as a means of assisting turns or slowing down rapidly.)

Stopping

The pilots may also use 'reverse thrust' on the engines to help slow down the aeroplane on the ground. The shuddering roar from the engines as this happens sometimes worries passengers, who think that something has gone wrong and the pilot is trying to take off again. Reverse thrust simply saves wear and tear on the brakes and tyres, but in many airlines current practice is not to use it if the landing has taken place on a long runway where there is plenty of room to slow down (it makes a lot of environmentally unfriendly noise).

Reverse thrust does not mean that the engine actually goes into reverse and blows out of the end which has been sucking. What happens is that when the pilots select reverse thrust in the cockpit, special doors or 'buckets' slide into place, deflecting the engines' exhausts forward at an angle. This is very effective in decelerating the aircraft when it is still travelling fast, but is less efficient as it slows down.

The wheel braking systems themselves are very powerful, and perfectly capable of bringing the aircraft to a stop without the use of reverse thrust from the engines. The braking systems will be at least duplicated and often triplicated, and 'anti-skid' – to prevent the wheels locking and hence skidding, if too much pressure is applied to the brakes – is virtually standard equipment on all airliners. The most modern aircraft have automatic braking systems, allowing the pilots to preselect a deceleration rate which will be activated on touchdown.

At the end of the landing run, all that remains is to taxi to the parking place or terminal building. As we do so, you will probably hear more 'noises off' as the pilots 'clean up' the aeroplane, retracting the slats and flaps, starting the auxiliary power unit, and so on. When the engines are shut down, you will hear the cabin crew leader telling his colleagues over the public address to 'disarm the slides' or 'doors to manual' – the signal to the rest of the crew to disable the automatic chutes, so that when the doors are opened the escape slides do not deploy.

The aircraft now becomes the focus of much activity: baggage trucks, catering vehicles, refuellers, engineers, cleaners and a host of others converge on it, all intent on getting it back into the air (and earning its keep) as soon as possible.

So that's it. Yet another routine flight. And now that you know a little more about what is going on, perhaps it's a bit less intimidating? OK. It was all very glib, wasn't it? If it's as straightforward as all that, WHY DO THE WRETCHED THINGS EVER CRASH? Are you strong enough for Part II, in which that question will be unflinchingly addressed? If so, read on . . .

PART II

The Chamber of Horrors

Turbulence

Turbulence is what causes an aircraft to shake, shudder, pitch, roll, bucket about and generally behave like a cork in a rough sea. It varies in intensity from the mildest of tremors running through the aeroplane, to extremely unpleasant stomach-churning drops and surges.

The first thing to remember is that, provided you have your seat belt fastened, it is unlikely that you will come to any harm. This is why sensible passengers keep their seat belt buckled, even loosely, throughout the flight.

The aeroplane will *not* fall apart, but passengers are sometimes hurt if unexpected turbulence is encountered and they are not strapped in. Then they can be flung out of their seats damaging themselves, fellow passengers, and bits of the expensive machine in which they are travelling.

This doesn't mean that you have to sit lashed tightly to your seat throughout the trip, gripping the armrests and too terrified even to go to the toilet. But when you *are* in your seat, 'clunk-click'. And if the 'fasten seat belts' sign is on, don't ignore it.

Damaging bits of the expensive machine

Turbulence can be caused by various phenomena, but at cruising heights it is most often associated with thunderstorms or very strong winds, called 'jet streams'.

The crew use the aircraft's radar to search ahead for thunderstorms and other clouds which might be turbulent, and then it is usually an easy matter to bypass the worst areas.

Clear Air Turbulence

A greater problem is so-called 'clear air turbulence' (CAT), which, as its name implies, occurs in clear air and is thus very difficult to spot in advance. By studying the weather charts before departure, the crew will know where CAT *may* be found, whilst other aircraft and air traffic control will broadcast advice alerting flights to known regions of CAT. Then the pilots of aircraft approaching the bumpy region can try various courses of action: they will switch on the 'fasten seat belts' sign, and probably announce over the public address system that the flight is approaching an area of turbulence. They will slow the aircraft down to a speed at which it will best 'ride' the turbulent air, and they may be able to climb, descend, or alter the route to avoid or reduce the problem.

If we do encounter clear air turbulence, it is often in the vicinity of a jet stream. A jet stream is a narrow 'tube' of very strong wind, with speeds reaching as high as 200 mph. On a meteorological chart these jet streams look rather like snakes writhing around the globe. Of course, a jet stream can be a good thing: if it is going in the same direction as the flight, we can often hitch a free ride in it with no turbulence at all. The turbulence is usually found on the edge of the jet stream, rather than actually within it.

If the worst comes to the worst and we do encounter CAT, it will probably not last long: 20 to 30 minutes is typical. As the aircraft bucks and heaves, it can be extremely uncomfortable for passengers, leaving their stomachs somewhere up on the roof of the cabin. If you are sitting by a window, you may also see the wings and engines flexing and bobbing about in what may appear to be a most alarming fashion. They are designed to do this: in general, the more flexible the wing, the more comfortable the ride. The engine pods, too, nod and sway, absorbing the bumps. Even in the worst turbulence, the screws and rivets which hold everything together won't come loose.

Modern aircraft are incredibly strong. During the

very extensive testing which all new aeroplanes undergo before they are flown, it is common for parts of the aircraft to be 'tested to destruction' in controlled experiments on the ground. If you ever have the chance to see photographs or film of wings undergoing this process, you will find it an amazing spectacle. The wings are bent upwards by hydraulic jacks until they finally break, but the angle they achieve *before* they fail is quite astonishing: far, far beyond anything they will ever encounter in flight.

To sum up, turbulence is sometimes very unpleasant in the passenger cabin, but it is not going to cause the aeroplane to break up. The crew will be doing everything they can to minimise the discomfort and to find smoother air. (Turbulence spills *our* coffee, too.)

Air Pockets

What if we hit an 'air pocket'? We won't – there is no such thing. The dropping sensation felt during turbulence is caused by a strong down-draught of air. The bumpiness results from flying from a down-draught into an up-draught, or vice versa, or when we are being buffeted by gusty winds, as may happen for a few minutes after take-off and before landing on a day when there are gales blowing on the ground.

Bombs and Hijacking

Unfortunately we live in an era in which uninvolved citizens are seen by terrorists as soft targets. This has led over the last two decades to the introduction of stringent – and often very inconvenient – security measures at airports. These are the first and main line of defence against the bomber and hijacker.

It would not be sensible to detail all the precautions which are taken to prevent terrorists gaining access to aircraft or being in a position to place bombs on board them. Most passengers will be aware of some of them: the screening of hand-baggage, body searches, etc, but other activities are taking place out of sight. These may include the X-raying of all luggage, the presence in the airport of armed and plain-clothes police, the use of intelligence agencies to pinpoint possible threats, and training given to airline staff to help them recognise the 'personality profile' of potentially unwelcome customers.

Regrettably, the terrorists are becoming more and more sophisticated, and unless the airlines resorted to screening measures which would be intolerable to most passengers (and which would probably cause the entire civil air transport system to seize up), there will always be a very slight risk that a determined, well-equipped group will be able to get a bomb or weapon onto an aircraft.

If a bomb *does* get aboard an aeroplane it is, of course, extremely serious, but not necessarily catastrophic. Many aircraft have survived explosions and landed safely – most famously, perhaps, one flown some years ago by a certain Far Eastern airline. This aircraft was twice the chosen venue for attempted suicide by hand grenade. On both occasions the unhappy traveller tried to blow himself up in the rear toilet, successfully achieving his aim, but also ripping a large hole in the cabin roof. On both occasions the aircraft landed with no further problem. (The same captain was flying the aircraft on both occasions.)

If a bomb is placed on an aircraft, it will probably be either amongst the baggage in the hold, or in the passenger cabin.

In the former case, if a warning is received in time, the crew will immediately make an emergency descent, depressurise the aircraft (to minimise stresses if the bomb does go off), and land at the nearest airport. The passengers will be told what is happening, and the cabin crew will instruct everyone on what to do.

From time to time, airlines receive bomb threats from mindless hoaxers. Most companies have a quick-reaction team which analyses the call and decides whether it merits serious consideration. In most cases, the answer is 'no' – it is quite apparent from the tone in which the 'warning' is given that it is some oafish prank. However, just occasionally there is sufficient doubt to justify further action. If the aircraft is on the ground, this means a thorough search of the aeroplane and its contents, including the passengers' baggage – a very tedious process which involves a long delay. If the aircraft is already in the air when such a threat – known as a 'specific threat' – is received, the airline will contact the captain by radio and advise him. The final decision will be up to the captain, but invariably he will decide to make an immediate diversion, followed by a thorough search of the aircraft – all adding up to a long delay. We are very definitely not amused by hoaxers.

Unfortunately, the events of 11 September 2001 blew away the theory that hijackers invariably want to ransom their captives for some concession and would thus allow the crew to remain at the controls and direct them to land somewhere, albeit probably not their original destination. Now we have to contend with a new breed of fanatic, careless of his own life, let alone those of his victims. The previous advice generally given to airline crews – to comply with the hijackers' demands as far as possible and to refrain at all costs from any 'Action Man' heroics – is now clearly no longer valid. Although these words are written only a few months after the horrific attacks on New York and Washington, it is fairly clear that the ground rules have changed radically.

Now, unless we are convinced otherwise beyond any reasonable doubt, we have to assume that we are being unwillingly appointed to the role of kamikazes. There has been considerable discussion in the pilot community as to how we should confront such a situation. Some quarters have suggested that pilots should be armed, but most of us are uncomfortable with this idea: the flight deck is the last place we want to stage a re-enactment of the gunfight at the OK Corral.

A number of airlines already fly with plain-clothes 'sky marshals' on board, some of whom are armed and some not. The presence of these guards is also controversial, because to be really effective, not even the operating crew should know who they are and where they are sitting. Some crews are unenthusiastic about the idea of having an armed but unknown security agent on the loose. Equally, the financial controllers are unhappy about the loss of a revenue-earning seat.

In the wake of 11 September, airlines are moving rapidly towards trying to isolate the cockpit by providing armoured – or at least strengthened – access doors to the flight deck, and possibly locating surveillance cameras in the cabin. There have also been some ludicrously impracticable ideas thrown around, ranging from quick-acting gasses to stun the passengers, to automatic control of the aircraft from the ground.

Of course, ground checks represent the main line of defence against the deranged and the evil, because it is infinitely preferable to prevent the problem from getting on board the aeroplane than it is to have to deal with it in the air. Anyone who has travelled through an airport recently will probably have noticed an increased level of vigilance.

Over the next few years, we can expect to see the introduction of some clever new technology. This will probably include rapid methods of electronic identification of the individual as he or she checks in. These will give airline personnel real time confirmation of the identity of the passenger and highlight any known details of a criminal or terrorist past or suspected links to undesirable groups or individuals. The person might then be refused passage or closely and discreetly monitored until he or she boards the flight, with subsequent special observation when on board.

With our eyes now wide open to the new threat, the flight crew can see that even without such drastic solutions as toting hardware more appropriate to late night cops-and-robbers movies, we have a number of cards up our sleeves. Since I have no idea how widely this little book may circulate in al Qaeda training camps, it would be unwise to publicise some of the things we could do that might help overcome a team of well-trained terrorists. However, there are two points to get across to the reader. The first is that you are *extremely* unlikely to find yourself involved a terrorist attack on board an aeroplane. Security on the ground has been beefed up, and everyone is now much more vigilant. But – the second point – in the unimaginable event that hijackers *do* strike when you are on board, *everyone* is now involved and must rise to the challenge. Hopefully, the crew will still be able to direct opposition to the attempted takeover. It is *essential* that everyone pitches in and does their bit: there are now no uninvolved bystanders. It was a US airline captain, operating one of the first services after the terrorist attacks, who made a remarkable announcement laying down the new 'ground rules'. After thanking his passengers for having the courage to board a flight so soon after the horrors of 11 September, he astonished everyone by continuing: 'If someone were to stand up, brandish something such as a plastic knife and say, "This is a hijacking," or words to that effect, here is what you should do: Every one of you should stand up and immediately throw things at that person – pillows, books, magazines, eyeglasses, shoes – anything that will throw him off balance and distract his attention. If he has a confederate or two, do the same with them. Most important, wrestle him to the floor and keep him there. We'll land the plane at the nearest airport and the authorities will take it from there. Remember, there will be one of him and maybe a few confederates, but there are two hundred of you . . .'

However melodramatic the captain's remarks may look in cold print, he was making a making a valid point. The message to keep in mind is that if the crew ask for your help, you must be prepared to do whatever you can: the situation is probably desperate.

But the other thing to keep even more in mind is that the chances of you ever being called upon to face such a situation are far more remote than those of, say, being involved in a hold-up as you visit your local bank. Flying is *still* a very safe and secure form of transport.

Air Rage

Antisocial behaviour has probably existed in aeroplanes since the first passengers wobbled aloft in flimsy string-

and-canvas contraptions early in the last century. But in those days sheer (justified) fear and the close proximity of a very *macho hombre* in leather jacket, helmet, and goggles probably prevented many overt displays of aggression. Anyway, those passengers were usually from the frightfully refined upper-classes, who might do horrid things to foxes, pheasants and cads, but who generally didn't swig lager from the can and then trash their immediate surroundings.

Flying, of course, has 'progressed'. No longer is it a remarkable and expensive adventure to travel from Croydon to Paris, rattling about in a wicker chair whilst a starched-collared steward serves smoked salmon and absinthe. Now, despite the glossy advertisements, the reality for most people is utterly dehumanising. Relatively cheap it may be to travel to destinations halfway across the globe, but at what a price in terms of treatment?

Sour-faced check-in staff, raucous fellow travellers in the bar, overcrowded departure lounges with fewer and worse facilities than an average cattle pen and aircraft seating designed by someone without even a passing acquaintance with the human frame. No wonder that there is a small number of people who 'flip'. Of course they *shouldn't*, but considering what airline passengers are subjected to, the air travel industry must accept some of the responsibility and examine (and implement) ways of reducing the stress involved, especially at airports.

That said, there is *never* any excuse for taking it out on the aircraft's crew. We have a very low tolerance threshold for oafish conduct on board, where the line between boorish behaviour and a threat to safety can easily be crossed.

In the first instance, we try to ensure that a drunken or abusive passenger never reaches the aircraft. Ground staff are under an obligation to inform the captain of any passenger they consider to be in an unfit state to travel, and it is the captain's prerogative to deny that person the right to board. However, human nature being what it is, ground staff sometimes turn a blind eye to the miscreant, in the hope that he (and it is usually, but not always, a 'he'), will soon be off their 'patch' and become someone else's problem.

Once we are airborne, the problem of an unruly passenger becomes much more serious. The cabin crew will have been given training in dealing with difficult predicaments and will do their best to defuse the situation. If things continue to deteriorate, the captain will be informed and will have to consider what options he has. One of these will almost certainly *not* be to come back and intervene personally. This reluctance is not due to sheer cowardice (although personally I find this a very compelling reason), but there is too much danger of a key member of the crew being put out of action.

If things in the back become really bad, the captain will probably decide to divert and have the cause of the problem removed from the aircraft. This will be a tedious procedure for everyone, but will probably be a better option than continuing for several hours to the original destination, with mayhem in the cabin. It is very rare that such diversions take place (the troublemaker usually backs off when it becomes apparent that everyone's patience has run out), but if it happens, just hope that the captain has chosen to land in one of those countries where jails are of the 'London Dungeon' variety.

What can you do if you find that you are sitting next to an obnoxious character? Divorcing him is not really a short-term solution. Ask one of the cabin crew if you can move, but do this *discreetly*, by ostensibly leaving your seat to go to the toilet, or passing the steward a note, so as not to exacerbate the problem or inflame your neighbour. If the flight is full, it may not be possible to move you, but in this case the cabin crew should start paying special attention to you.

If the cabin crew, especially an all-female crew, ask for your assistance to subdue a violent and unruly person, please pile in and help. If a real fracas has broken out, you and everyone else on board that aircraft are now definitely at risk: the hooligan *must* be controlled before anyone or anything gets seriously damaged.

However, statistics show that you are very unlikely to have your journey marred by exposure to antisocial behaviour: only one in 66,000 passengers is classed as unruly, with only one passenger in four million becoming seriously disruptive.

The Aircraft

Structural Failure

Passengers sometimes watch as several hundred people clamber aboard one of the big jets. They see tonnes of baggage and cargo being loaded into the holds, and they wonder how an aircraft can carry all that weight. Will the wings come off or the bottom fall out? Will it be able to take off?

Modern aircraft are both extremely strong and extremely powerful. They are designed to withstand conditions way outside those which they will ever meet during their lifetime (which may be 30–40 years). Throughout that life, they are closely monitored by engineers, with the inspections becoming more searching as the aircraft gets older.

Even if it is loaded up to its maximum allowed weight, there is still a wide margin of safety in hand. As we have seen earlier, an aircraft must be able to continue with a safe take-off following the failure of one of its engines at the most critical moment.

Both the cabin and floors are very strongly stressed. The cabin floor has to withstand such contingencies as a large lady standing on it in high heels during turbulence – the pressure exerted by a tiny heel in such circumstances can be immense!

The hold floors are equally strong, and careful attention is paid to the loading of the freight and baggage to ensure that the correct balance of the aircraft is maintained and that it is all safely tied down. (As an aside, we do carry some remarkable cargoes. A few years ago, the writer flew out a holidaymaker who had decided to bring his car with him – a Mercedes. A week later, he decided to send for his other car – a Rolls-Royce. Both fitted neatly into our hold.)

Engine Failure

We have seen in the previous section that a single engine failure, even at a critical point during the take-off, is easily manageable. Equally, the failure of an engine en route – even over a mountain range or in mid-ocean – will have been taken into consideration in advance and the crew will know whether they should continue or turn back. Over the ocean, a twin-engined aircraft must always be within a specified flying time, on *one* engine, of an airport where it could make an emergency landing.

But supposing *all* the engines fail? This *has* happened. At least twice, Boeing 747 jumbos have inadvertently flown into clouds of volcanic ash which have clogged up the engines and stopped them. This must have been an extremely frightening experience for all concerned, but on both occasions the crew managed to get several engines working again and made safe landings. There have also been at least three incidents in which both motors of twin-engined airliners have failed. Again, on each occasion the crew managed to land the aircraft successfully due to their piloting skills, and perhaps also to a measure of luck – especially in the case of an incident in the summer of 2001, when an Airbus A330 developed a serious leak and ran out of fuel over the Atlantic at night, fortuitously within gliding distance of the Azores.

The point, however, is that in the highly unlikely case of all engines failing, everything is *not* lost. Most aeroplanes glide surprisingly well, and – unless the odds were really stacked against you – there would be a very good chance of pulling off a successful (although not necessarily dignified) landing.

Doors
The positions of all the aircraft's doors are displayed in the cockpit, so that we can ensure that they are properly closed before we start the engines. The doors cannot be

opened in flight, so there is no chance of anyone opening one and falling out!

Fuel

Will the aircraft run out of fuel if the winds are stronger than expected, or the flight is delayed?

Before departure the crew must ensure that sufficient fuel is on board for the aircraft to fly to its destination, taking into account the expected wind. There must also be enough fuel for the aircraft to make an approach to the destination airport and if – for some reason – it can't land, it must then be able to go to another, alternate airport and to circle overhead *that* airfield for 30 minutes before landing. A 'pad' (typically 5 per cent) is then added to all that fuel and the resulting total is the *minimum* which must be on board at departure. Of course, the captain is perfectly entitled to take as much extra fuel as he wants if the weather is bad – even leaving passengers or freight behind if necessary.

Throughout the flight, the crew, aided by computer predictions of how the flight should be progressing, keep a very sharp eye on the amount of fuel remaining. If at any point it seems that the reserves are dropping too low, then the crew will divert to an en route airport for refuelling (a so-called 'tech stop').

Since tech stops inconvenience passengers and cause the airline extra costs, aircrew prefer to take a conservative view of weather forecasts and route congestion, and load sufficient fuel to preclude any possibility of having to refuel en route.

Even if something unexpected happens as the aircraft approaches its destination, such as congestion causing a long delay before landing, the crew will decide to divert to the alternate airport well before the fuel becomes embarrassingly low.

The fuel used by jet aircraft, incidentally, is a form of paraffin. It has a high 'flash point', the temperature at which it will ignite. Readers of a certain seniority may remember a dramatic publicity film made by a British airline many years ago, in which the chairman stood in a puddle of jet aviation fuel, dropping lighted matches into it (and challenging his competitors to do the same with the more volatile fuels which they were, at that time, using). The chairman remained un-immolated.

The Pilots

'How do I know if they're any good?' The writer's natural modesty makes this an awkward topic, so let's look at it purely factually.

FLYING? NO FEAR!

To be a pilot you need a reasonable standard of education and health, good coordination, and a certain mental outlook. The rest is training.

Civilian pilots obtain this training in different ways. Some come from a military flying background, while others are the products of the civilian training system. This latter is very expensive: it costs someone embarking on a flying career tens of thousands of pounds to obtain their basic licence to be a professional (rather than recreational) pilot. The course which leads to this licence lasts about a year and involves a study of all aspects of aviation, including aerodynamics, thermodynamics, meteorology, radio, law, and a host of other subjects. At the same time, the student will be undergoing flying instruction, progressing from simple single-engine aircraft, to twin-engine aeroplanes with more sophisticated instruments, which he or she must learn to fly without looking out of the cockpit. The culmination of the course is a series of flying and written exams, in which the pass mark is very high.

Many would-be pilots can't afford such a course, and either can't get into, or don't want to join the military. If they are very lucky, they may find an airline to sponsor their training, in return for a certain number of years' service with that company. But others will have to embark on the sheer hard graft of the 'self-improver' route: getting a private pilot's licence (costing several thousand pounds, this licence only allows you to fly for pleasure, not for remuneration), then scraping together enough hours of flying to become an instructor (and getting paid at last, albeit often only a pittance). Working thus, the pilot will build up his experience until he or she reaches the minimum required to be allowed to take the examinations for a commercial pilot's licence (CPL).

A CPL allows someone to act as a co-pilot on a large aeroplane like an airliner. He or she will be fully qualified to fly the aeroplane, and in routine airline operations the captain and the co-pilot take it in turns to do the take-off and the landing, (although if the weather is bad or the flying is likely to be particularly demanding, the captain will take over). So a co-pilot is, in effect, undergoing an 'apprenticeship' – he or she is a 'captain-in-waiting'.

To qualify for the licence which allows you to be a captain requires more experience and the passing of yet more exams. After that, the airline itself will set stringent standards for aspiring commanders: it isn't about to entrust just anyone with millions of dollars' worth of hardware and customers. The route to a civil aviation command is long and hard.

Few other professions are as rigorously checked as that of a pilot. Each individual typically undergoes at least seven medical or competency checks each year, all of which must be passed. The medicals become more searching as you get older, and include sight, hearing, and cardiac checks.

The competency checks are carried out by Cruel and Sadistic Instructors or CSIs (known to their faces as check-pilots, training captains, or sir).

At least once per year each pilot will find a training captain sitting in on a routine flight, observing the captain's or co-pilot's performance. These are comparatively 'friendly' events, since the presence of witnesses (passengers) restricts the training captain's more barbaric instincts. He is really waiting to get his victims into the 'simulator'.

Simulators are exact reproductions of the aircraft's cockpit which are mounted on hydraulically operated legs to impart a sense of motion. They are equipped with sophisticated visual systems (so that you can 'see' through the windscreens). The whole contraption is controlled by computers which are capable of reproducing the flying characteristics of a real aeroplane with uncanny accuracy.

They could be fun, like some giant arcade game, but they're not: they are equipped with a station at which the Cruel and Sadistic Instructor sits, confronted by buttons allowing him to introduce an almost infinite variety of catastrophes into the proceedings. A simulator in the hands of a CSI is, quite simply, a high tech version of a medieval torture chamber. An airline pilot usually has to undergo at least four sessions in this device each year.

A typical simulator session starts with a fire and engine failure on take-off from a runway which (of course) is shrouded in fog (thus making a quick return to land difficult or impossible). Thereafter things progress rapidly from bad to worse, as the hydraulics disintegrate, electrical power fails, etc. Needless to say, the autopilot isn't working and the co-pilot will have been told to display the maximum level of incompetence of which he is capable. All this goes on for about three or four hours, which is probably contrary to the Geneva Convention.

The CSI, of course, enjoys himself hugely. When not engaged in pressing buttons to heap further disasters upon the wilting shoulders of the wretched victim, he will be making copious notes for use at the de-briefing session which rounds the whole thing off (this, in itself, makes the average interrogation centre seem like a charm school).

Amazingly, most pilots recuperate from this bestial treatment surprisingly quickly – often after the first round in the bar afterwards. By the second round, many even begin to feel that it has been a good thing: if they can handle *that*, then anything that goes wrong in real life should be plain sailing.

(*Addendum*: The writer now finds himself in a bit of a dilemma. Shortly after writing the above paragraphs a few years ago, he, too, was elevated to the distinguished pantheon of training captains. He can now see clearly that, far from being 'cruel and sadistic', training captains actually embody all that is finest in the human spirit. Of all their exemplary qualities, arguably the greatest is their extraordinary patience as they go about the thankless task of trying to impart even the tiniest scraps of their own unbounded skill and wisdom to the unreceptive 'blobbies' with whom they are forced to share a flight deck or simulator. A measure of the training captain's benign nature is that the writer has allowed the previous calumnies to stand uncensored.)

Other Fears

Ditching

What if we have to land on water? There have been very few emergency landings on water by modern airliners – 'ditchings' as they are called. There was a successful one in the Caribbean many years ago and more recently, a hijacked Ethiopian aircraft ran out of fuel over the Indian Ocean. The crew's extremely skilful efforts to ditch the unpowered aeroplane were tragically wrecked when one of the hijackers grabbed the controls at the last moment. Nevertheless, many people survived the catastrophe.

Airliner manufacturers carry out tests with models and computer simulations which offer pilots guidance on the best way to 'ditch' if they should ever have to, and provided the aircraft survives the impact relatively undamaged, they should float quite well.

All flights which will fly over the sea must be equipped with life jackets for the passengers and crew, and life rafts if they will spend many hours over water. (In passing, some people take the exhortation that '*your* life jacket is under your seat' a bit literally. It is only yours for the duration of the trip. Unlike the in-flight magazine, they are not to be taken home afterwards!)

Fire

The aircraft is equipped with sensors to detect smoke or heat, and these will immediately alert the crew to any outbreak of fire in the engines, holds, or cabin.

If an engine catches fire, there is only one source which will sustain the flames – fuel. The fire drill which the crew will carry out cuts off the fuel supply to the engine.

In theory, this alone should put out the fire. But built-in fire extinguishers will also be discharged. Engine fires are very rare indeed (although dealing with them is regularly practised in the simulator).

Cabin fires are rarely serious, simply because they are quickly spotted and dealt with. They too are thankfully very uncommon, but those which do occur are usually caused by careless smokers dropping cigarettes or accidentally setting something alight. There is always a strict rule against smoking in the toilets, because it is easy for a fire to start if a smoker drops a cigarette into one of the waste bins there which are full of discarded paper towels.

The toilets are equipped with sensitive smoke detectors. If you are not allowed to smoke in the cabin for any reason, *do not* sneak off to the toilet for a quick drag: the alarm will sound and you will get a richly deserved roasting from the crew.

The cabin crew are thoroughly trained in fighting fires. There are numerous fire extinguishers located around the cabin, and the crew also have special protective and breathing equipment available to enable them to tackle even a serious blaze.

Fires in aircraft cargo holds can be disastrous, and several fatal accidents have resulted from such incidents. The main line of defence against cargo hold fires is preventing hazardous items getting onto the aircraft in the first place. There is a long list of restricted items which cannot be carried on passenger flights, or which must be specially packed if they are to be flown.

It is less easy to control what passengers put in their suitcases. Did *you* know, for example, that you should not carry mercury thermometers or barometers? If they break, even tiny amounts of mercury can react with the metal skin of the aircraft and cause immense damage. And non-safety matches can ignite spontaneously and cause a fire in your suitcase, which can then spread to other baggage and freight.

If a fire does break out in a cargo hold or amongst the baggage, it will be detected by sensors in those areas. The holds themselves are usually either airtight, so any fire will quickly be starved of oxygen and go out, or they are equipped with fire extinguishers which can be discharged from the cockpit.

Stalling

'Stalling' is what happens if an aeroplane flies too slowly or too fast, so that the airflow over the wings becomes so seriously disrupted that they can no longer provide the lift to keep the aeroplane airborne. At this stage, the machine takes on many of the flying characteristics of a brick. Pilots take great care to ensure that the aircraft never comes anywhere near to these upper or lower limits of the 'flight envelope'. In modern aeroplanes, there are a variety of devices and warnings to prompt the crew to the fact that they are approaching a stalled condition. In fact, the very latest aircraft (for example, the Airbus family) are 'stall-proof': their computers will ultimately override any input from the pilots which could lead to the aircraft becoming stalled.

On take-off and landing the aeroplane will be flying at about 25–30 per cent above the stalling speed, with a similar margin below the 'high speed stall' being maintained during the cruise.

Even in the extremely unlikely event that the aircraft does, somehow, get into a stall, the recovery from it is quick and easy (and another of the manoeuvres which are practised in the simulator).

I Am Not In Control

This is a very common reaction amongst apprehensive flyers. Probably the best way of coming to terms with this feeling is to take a philosophical approach. An airline crew is very highly trained and you are in good hands. You probably do not worry too much about being in a train or bus, although you are not in control of these forms of transport either (and far less money will have been spent on training the crew and servicing the vehicle).

I Can't Get Out

Civil airliners do not carry parachutes: for a start, we cannot open the doors in flight (the air pressure inside the cabin makes this impossible, even if the door mechanism was operated) and anyway it is highly unlikely that untrained passengers could make a successful parachute descent even if they had time to put on parachutes in an emergency and could 'bail out'. So although you cannot get out, you are in a very safe 'cocoon' whilst you are on board.

Safety Record

Before we look at why mishaps occur, let's get the accident rate in context. Far too often following an accident, lurid tabloid headlines obscure the fact that such events are extraordinarily remote.

For much of the following information, I am indebted to *Flight International*, the world's leading aviation magazine.

The world's airlines make about one million flights

each month, carrying over a billion passengers annually. Over the last decade there have been about 44 fatal airline accidents each year, in which just over a thousand people died. But during this period, the number of flights has risen by 42 per cent and the number of passengers travelling is up by 50 per cent, so in real terms, aviation safety continues to improve from year to year.

This is an extremely good record by any standards (although you will find no complacency in the flying world). Your chances of being involved in an accident when you board an aircraft are very, very small indeed.

As a comparison, about 80,000 people are killed on the roads of Europe each year.

Frequently Asked Questions

How Do Aeroplanes Fly?

If you hold a piece of paper by one edge horizontally in front of you with the thumb and forefinger of each hand, the end the furthest away from you will droop down. If you now blow gently over the curve thus formed, the paper will lift up. This is why aeroplanes fly.

The wings of an aircraft are shaped rather like the drooping piece of paper: the upper surface is curved – more towards the front than the back – whilst the lower surface is flat. As the wing is pushed along (the function of the engines), the air passing over the upper surface has to move faster than the air going underneath, because it has further to go. This creates a lower pressure above the wing; hence the wing is 'sucked' upwards – a process called 'lift'.

In order to turn, the wings must be tilted (merely moving the rudder at the back would cause the aircraft to 'skid' round corners in a most uncomfortable manner). So turning is achieved through the use of 'ailerons', small flaps on the rear of each wing which move in opposite directions on each side of the aircraft. These effectively alter the curvature of the wing to which they are attached, so one wing moves up and the other down, creating a 'banked' condition. The 'lift' is now not only working directly upwards to overcome gravity, it is also pulling the aeroplane left or right.

This is a pretty simplistic explanation of what is going on and the writer won't entertain any correspondence from outraged aerodynamicists. It applies to most types of aeroplane except Concorde. Concorde wings work on a principle of digitally enhanced macrobiotic vortices or something similar. Don't even *try* to understand how it flies: merely pay your money and feel privileged to sit in one of the most beautiful pieces of technology ever to rattle your windows.

(Just as an aside, in one of his earlier professional exams, the writer was asked to describe the aerodynamic process by which an aircraft turns. Re-reading his solution just before 'time up', he found that he had conclusively and scientifically proved that it is absolutely impossible for an aeroplane to turn. He passed the exam.)

Is There A Safest Place To Sit?

There is a popular myth that says that sitting at the rear of aircraft is safer than sitting at the front. The UK's

Civil Aviation Authority is not aware of any statistical evidence showing this to be the case, although the flight data recorder – the so-called 'black box' (actually it is usually a red one) is often located in the tail section.

If you do sit in the rear, the down side is that this is sometimes the smoking section (you are much more likely to die of smoking-related problems than in an air crash), and the rear of some aircraft tend to sway more than the front end in turbulence. It may also be noisier at the back, especially in rear-engined types. Large, wide-bodied aircraft seem to offer better chances of survival in an accident, perhaps because they have a lot of 'structure' to absorb impact forces.

If it makes you feel better, you can check in early and ask to be seated in one of the rows adjacent to an emergency exit (these also have the added bonus of extra legroom, although the seats don't recline). These rows are generally restricted to able-bodied passengers.

The most important contribution you can make to your safety when in an aircraft is to notice where the emergency exits are (not just the door by which you entered the aeroplane), and pay attention to the cabin crew's pre-take off safety briefing. In the extremely unlikely event of anything going wrong, don't panic, and do exactly as you are told by the crew without delay. If the accident is survivable, your chances of getting out are very high provided you keep calm, know what to do, and follow instructions.

Which Are the Safest Airlines?

You pay for the libel lawyer, and I'll tell you which airlines I would avoid! In fact, most airlines that you are likely to consider in your travel plans are OK. European and North American airlines generally maintain a high standard. Size is not necessarily an indication of quality: many small airlines operate to very high standards. Of all international airlines, those based in Australia have maintained an exceptionally good record over a very long time.

Some Asian airlines, and some from the Republics established after the break-up of the Soviet Union, have acquired dubious reputations. In the case of the latter, economic hardship seems to be playing a role, with some airlines operating obsolete equipment which may be poorly maintained.

In the Far East, a major problem appears to be the cultural character of the pilots: the regional emphasis on hierarchy and respect for one's superior seems to deter co-pilots from challenging the actions of the captain, with the captains for their part sometimes exercising a domineering attitude in the cockpit. In the West, such attitudes have for many years been recognised as unhealthy, and great efforts have been made to ensure that a climate exists on the flight deck where any member of the crew can voice his or her concern at what a colleague is doing.

Despite the occasional screaming headline in the tabloid press, there are no 'rogue' aircraft types. *All* airliners are exhaustively tested before they receive government approval to carry passengers.

Charter and 'low cost' airlines should not be seen as less safe than the major carriers.

'Delay Due To Technical Reasons.' What Does This Really Mean?

This is the 'catch all' excuse airlines often use to cover a delay, without perhaps realising the distress this can cause to an apprehensive passenger. It can cover everything from a major breakdown in one of the aircraft's systems, to the fact that the pilot has had a puncture on his way to the airport. It is a very irritating excuse; just marginally better than being given no reason at all for a delay.

The most important thing to remember is that if the aeroplane needs fixing, it *will* be fixed before you fly in it. The crew have families, too, and will know more about the extent of the problem than you do, as you sit frustratedly in the departure lounge. The crew will not be fobbed off with anything less than a fully flyable aircraft.

However, on those rare occasions when a system defect appears shortly before departure, the main problem can be in determining how long it will take to fix. The engineers first have to locate the source of the trouble and then do something about it. If something isn't working as it should, the cause may not be immediately apparent: it may simply be a case of plugging in a replacement 'black box', or it may require the removal of lots of bits to get at the offending part. Engineers are very loath to commit themselves until they are sure of what they are up against, and this lack of 'hard' information to pass to waiting passengers is often a cause of much frustration.

Can the Passengers Unbalance an Aircraft?

No. Very occasionally we ask passengers to sit in particular seat rows to optimise the balance of the aircraft for take-off, but once we are airborne there is no problem. The aircraft's trimming system is very powerful (it moves the entire 'horizontal stabiliser', the small 'wings' at the back of the aircraft), so there is no way that even such phenomena as a queue for the toilet or people walking up and down could affect the aeroplane's balance.

Computers – Can They Go Wrong?

As the enlightened reader will realise, there is no such thing as an *in*animate object. Everything has a character of its own, usually malevolent. There is no better example of this truism than computers, as anyone knows who owns a PC and has watched an entire morning's work disappear from the screen simply because you have inadvertently pressed the wrong button. Can the same thing happen with all this wizardry aboard the aircraft?

Great care is taken to prevent any such catastrophe, first of all by ensuring that the weakest link – the pilots – cannot get access to the software (the stuff that makes the computers work). These programs are designed, produced and tested in places called Silicon Valleys by people of mind-boggling intellect, who are not supposed to goof-off on the job. It is the task of those right-stuff manufacturers' test pilots to ensure that the programs really are error-free during the prolonged trials which take place before an aircraft enters service.

Most of the computers on board, especially the most vital ones, also check themselves and will let the crew know if they are not happy with what they find. For example, the programs of the flight control computers in the latest generation of airliners are written in different languages by different companies (which are not allowed to communicate with each other). The computers then check that these programs match *exactly* before they execute the resulting commands. It is thus highly unlikely that a serious error could be duplicated within this system.

Ultimately, of course, there is always that little red button on the control column which, if pressed, cuts out virtually all the automatics and leaves the pilots in full control. Computers *hate* that little button, and its mere existence is usually enough to keep them in line.

Are There Any Simple Ideas Which Would Make Flying Safer?

Fitting retractable 'lap and diagonal' seat belts would offer much better protection in the event of an accident than the simple lap straps which are currently used. (Rear-facing seats would be even better, but are strongly resisted by passengers.) Why aren't they fitted? Because the first airline to do so would risk giving the impression that it was less safe than its competitors.

Strengthening overhead lockers would help to prevent them coming loose in an accident. This area is being worked on by aircraft manufacturers and government air safety organisations.

Establishing duty-free facilities on arrival, rather than on departure, would prevent hundreds of potential fragmentation and incendiary devices (bottles of spirits) being brought on board every flight. Some enlightened airports already practise this; why don't they all?

Why do Aircraft Crash?

Statistically, the main cause remains human error. Although manufacturers are continually making airliners easier and safer to fly and maintain, whilst human beings are involved in the chain, from design to manufacturing to maintenance to flying, errors will occasionally creep in. Most often these are of little consequence: just very occasionally, they are catastrophic.

You can minimise your exposure to such errors by flying with airlines which enjoy a sound reputation and which fly modern, well-equipped and well-maintained aircraft. Most western airlines fall into this category, but so do many from so-called Third World countries (which is why the *worldwide* accident rate is so low).

Typically about 65 per cent of accidents are put down to human error, although in the past this has sometimes been used as a convenient 'catch all' term through which blame can be pinned on a scapegoat, whilst strongly contributory errors of omission and commission remain obscured.

Accidents almost always result from a chain of events, which may start quite innocuously. If the chain can be broken at almost any point, the accident will be averted.

In recent years, increasing attention has been paid to the interface between man and machine, human factors, and crew resource management (HF and CRM). Or in plain language: 'Why does the right stuff sometimes turn out to be the wrong stuff?' Much of the thrust to improve flight safety now involves psychology, with crews learning how to interact and communicate better, and to recognise developing situations which could lead to problems. Hard evidence shows that crews that have received this form of training perform better than those that have not.

The next main cause of fatal accidents (about 37 per cent) is 'controlled flight into terrain' (CFIT) – the flight of a perfectly serviceable aircraft into the ground. Very often this involves at least some degree of human error, and HF and CRM training seem likely to bring about marked improvements in this area.

FLYING? NO FEAR!

Recent advances in digital technology have allowed the introduction of a system: Enhanced Ground Proximity Warning System (EGWPS), which gives pilots early warning that they are approaching terrain, displaying this information in a compelling and readily understandable manner, which can mean the difference between life and a hole in the hillside.

Human error and CFIT are followed by weather and technical failure in the league of causes of accidents. Hijacking and sabotage account for a tiny proportion of incidents (for example, in a recent year the five deaths attributed to hijacking were all of the terrorists themselves).

Flying can never be 100 per cent safe. (Nor indeed can anything else; life itself has, after all, been described as a 'terminal condition'.) However, as I hope this book has shown, you are probably safer in an aeroplane than when undertaking almost any other activity.

Part III

Conquering Your Fear The Natural Way

Dr George Georgiou, Ph.D.

I believe that it is very important for anyone who suffers from anxiety or phobias to understand fully what is happening to them during an anxiety attack. Understanding the symptoms is the first step to being able to combat them.

Many people who have anxiety attacks feel that they are in impending danger and fear dying of a heart attack, cerebral vascular accident or some other wicked ailment.

The reason for this is that the subjective feelings of anxiety, particularly at their peak, are so frightening and awesome that anyone would feel like death is knocking on their door. Gaining a detailed understanding of what is happening to your mind and body during an anxiety attack will facilitate your ability to control the situation. It will also help put into perspective those distorted feelings of impending danger that surface, hence alleviating the intensity of the attack.

I think it is also important to clarify from the very beginning that anxiety, however acute, *cannot*, and *will not* kill you. There is absolutely no way that an anxiety attack can do any serious physical harm to the body. It can certainly make you feel extremely uncomfortable and fearful, but on a physical level it can do nothing harmful.

Most of the feelings and sensations that we have during an anxiety attack are due to stimulation of part of the nervous system called the 'autonomic nervous system' (ANS). There are two parts to this system, the sympathetic part which basically switches the body 'on' and prepares it to deal with any perceived danger, real or otherwise, and the parasympathetic part which basically switches the body 'off' and brings it back to its normal state. Immediately after an anxiety attack, which usually lasts a few minutes, the parasympathetic part of the ANS is triggered and returns the body back to its normal state. So let us look in brief how and why your body reacts when it is turned 'on' and is in a state of anxious turmoil.

Anxiety

The Dreaded Enemy

An actor who goes on stage after many rehearsals and cannot utter a word because his mind has gone blank.

An accomplished pianist finds that his fingers have gone stiff as he begins playing at an international concert.

An intelligent student taking an exam cannot think or write as her mind is streaming with irrelevant thoughts.

Each of these mishaps is characteristic of the condition commonly called *anxiety*. One of the paradoxical features of acute anxiety is that the person seems to bring on unwittingly what he fears or detests the most. In fact, the greater the fear of a specific situation or event, the more likely it seems to the sufferer that it will actually happen.

There are various components of anxiety, namely: (1) a physiological reaction of sweating, increased heart rate and dizziness; (2) various negative thoughts such as 'I am going to disgrace myself;' (3) a wish to avoid the anxiety-provoking situation; (4) feelings of terror and calamity; (5) behavioural changes such as losing balance or not being able to speak.

Phobias: Anxiety At Its Worst

Phobia refers to a specific kind of fear and is defined as 'an unreasonable fear of a particular object or situation.' The key phrase is 'unreasonable fear', as everyone has fears of certain things. A person confronted by a venomous rattlesnake will undoubtedly be afraid, and justifiably so. However, a person faced with a small, harmless grass snake or slow-worm has no need to be overtly afraid and anxious. A phobia is characterised by an intense desire to avoid the feared situation, and evokes anxiety when one is exposed to that situation.

Next to alcohol abuse, phobias are the most common psychological disorders. In hierarchical order, fear of snakes comes top of the list, followed by fear of heights, fear of mice, and then fear of flying. Approximately 20 per cent of people are afraid of flying, but it is only a small percentage of these that find the fear so incapacitating that they avoid flying altogether. Such people will probably not be reading this little book!

People who tend to react with violent anxiety before and during an aeroplane trip are probably the ones who will avoid flying at all costs. Some fear they will suffocate on the aeroplane, others that they will lose control of themselves in public, and a significant proportion of aeroplane phobias are related to agoraphobia, the fear of being trapped in a closed space. More commonly, however, the flying phobic fears the aeroplane will crash and that he will be killed, even though flying is one of the safest forms of transport.

Phobic Symptoms: How Does The Body Cope?

The symptoms of anxiety tend to trigger many different reactions in the body: psychological, emotional, behavioural and physiological. Some of the psychological symptoms may include: difficulty in concentration; fear of losing control; inability to control thinking; confusion; inability to recall important things; sentences broken or disconnected; fear of dying or stuttering

It is important to note the person's fear of injury or death, however, unlikely this may be in reality. It is usually this fear that causes the anxiety which generates the physical symptoms, which in turn feeds the fear that you are going to have a heart attack or stroke or whatever.

CONQUER YOUR FEAR OF FLYING

It is *only a fear* – you are *not* going to have a heart attack or die. It requires much more than anxiety to kill us!

The person who suffers from anxiety and phobia is indulging in faulty thinking. Typically, they 'catastrophise' – dwelling on the worst possible outcome of a situation. The anxious person usually exaggerates the possible consequences of an event. An example of this behaviour would be a preoccupation with the possibility of the aeroplane crashing and of being killed. The chance of this happening is one in millions, since flying is such an extraordinarily safe way of travelling as we have seen earlier in this book.

Apart from faulty thinking, perhaps the most frightening aspect of the panic attack is the loss of control that the individual has always taken for granted. He or she has to struggle to retain or regain voluntary control over focusing, concentration, attention, and action. At times, the difficulty in focusing extends to a sense that he is losing consciousness, although actual loss of consciousness is rare.

Of course, the most striking characteristic of the panic attack is the feeling of being engulfed by uncontrollable anxiety. This feeling has been described by many of my patients as 'unending pain' and 'the worst experience of my life – I thought I was going to die!'

The physiological symptoms reflect a readiness of the total organism for self-protection. Some of these physiological symptoms include: palpitations, faintness, shortness of breath, insomnia, tremors, nausea, pressure to urinate and 'hot and cold' spells.

The body generally prepares itself for the 'flight or fight' reaction that characterises phobic anxiety states. The heart and cardiovascular system will therefore increase their output to provide more blood to the muscles and other organs, the pupils dilate, the gut slows down and so on.

These bodily sensations are often 'catastrophised' by the anxious person. Thus:

CONQUER YOUR FEAR OF FLYING

Symptom	Interpreted as:
Abdominal or chest pain + faintness	Heart attack!
Changes in mental functioning (difficulty in focusing, 'fogginess', depersonalisation, etc)	Going mad!
Difficulty in catching breath	'I will stop breathing and die!"
Faintness	Impending coma and death!
Generalised sense of loss of control over internal sensations	Uncontrollable or bizarre behaviour!

It is again important to realise that these uncomfortable and painful symptoms *cannot* cause heart attacks, strokes, madness, apnoea (stopping breathing) or total loss of control. At worst they will make you feel extremely uncomfortable and agitated, and you will not be able to keep focused and concentrated on any one task. *But that is all!*

Coping Techniques

Today there are many techniques used by scientists to deal with the dreaded symptoms of anxiety. There are psychological techniques that focus on changing the way that the person perceives his anxiety (cognitive therapies), the way a person feels about the perceived threat (affective therapies) and the way a person behaves (behavioural therapies).

There is also another natural approach, which is of particular interest to me as a biologist, nutritionist and natural medicine practitioner, and this is the natural, alternative approach. This involves using a variety of nutritional supplements such as vitamins, amino acids and minerals, combined with an adequate diet to help control and alleviate anxiety symptoms. One can also use the Bach Flower Remedies, which I will discuss in more detail later.

Although this is a huge subject which could fill many volumes, let me outline a few techniques which can be used by an anxious person sitting on the seat of an aeroplane. These include doing easy relaxation exercises, using positive images to replace negative and frightening ones, and possibly using a variety of nutritional

supplements and Bach Flower Remedies which can help
a person relax. Let us begin by examining a simple
technique that can be used from the comfort of your
seat for changing and modifying those negative images
which spark a lot of the anxiety.

Positive Imagery – Think Positive, Feel Positive

For a long time now psychologists have realised that
undesirable visual images often stimulate negative
thoughts, which in turn provoke anxiety and tension.
Thinking that the plane will fall any minute due to an
engine failure or some other mechanical problem is
bound to make you feel tense and anxious. The opposite
is also true; if we can focus on pleasant, positive images
(sunbathing, being with our favourite partner, being
loved by a friend or relative), then this will tend to create
more positive thoughts and maintain a state of inner
relaxation. The identification of this cognitive process
is a positive step forward towards gaining mastery of
your phobic anxiety.

For example, suppose you are beginning to have
negative thoughts about the aeroplane crashing. You can
see this clearly on your mind's 'television' screen. What
you must try to do is to change the channel. Flick the

internal 'switch' and select a more appropriate programme.

Close your eyes and try to tune into your breathing. If you are breathing too fast, slow down and take a few slow deep breaths. Now try to focus on a soothing scene:

As you get more experienced, you can change the image to one you like better. It is difficult to have a positive image in mind, whilst concomitantly having a negative one too. So the more positive images you have, the more relaxed you will be.

Imagine yourself lying comfortably on a golden, sandy beach. It is late afternoon and the sun is warm but not scorching. The beach is quiet with very few people to disturb you. There are a couple of children quietly playing volleyball, and a young couple next to you really enjoying each other's company. You can feel the sun's heat penetrating your body deeply and soothing those tense and aching muscles. You can feel the heat entering your head through your nose and slowly sifting through you until it exits through your feet, taking away all the tensions. You are really relaxed and enjoying the comfortable state of being at peace with yourself. You can hear the rush of the waves in rhythm with your breathing, deep and slow. You can hear the cry of the seagulls hovering above a small fishing trawler, and the sounds of the children playing volleyball. You can hear all these sounds, but they are in the background, far from your immediate concentration. Lie on the beach in a state of deep relaxation and inner peace for a couple of hours. Enjoy the total peace of mind.

Quieting Reflex

Another easy relaxation technique that has been explained by Dr Terry Looker and Dr Olga Gregson in their book on stress is called the 'quieting reflex'. It is very simple, and only takes a few seconds to implement, but can have excellent results in the alleviation of anxiety and tension.

Close your eyes. Pinpoint in your mind what is annoying or stressing you. Say to yourself slowly, 'Relax, relax. I'm not going to let this get to me.'

Smile to yourself. You can practice smiling to yourself without showing a smile on your face. Actually going through the motions of smiling has been shown to improve your mood too, as it releases chemicals in the brain that are associated with pleasure and contentment.

Breathe in, to the count of three while imagining that the air comes in through holes in your feet. Feel the sensation of warmth and heaviness flowing through your body, starting at your feet and ending at your head.

Breathe out to the count of three. Visualise your breath passing through your body from your head and out through the holes in your feet. Feel the warmth and heaviness flow through your body. Let your muscles relax, let the jaw, tongue and shoulders go limp.

Now open your eyes and resume your normal activity.

The Nutritional Approach

It was Hippocrates, the father of physicians, who wisely said 2,500 years ago: 'Let food be thy medicine and medicine be thy food.'

It's unfortunate that very few modern-day physicians have taken heed of this. Hippocrates was using natural ingredients to allow the body to heal itself, which is called the 'orthomolecular' approach to medicine. By providing those molecules or nutrients that the body lacks such as vitamins, minerals, fatty acids and amino acids along with an optimum diet, it is possible to restore the body's physical, psychological and spiritual balance and health. The opposite approach, widely practised by the majority of the medical profession, is the 'toximolecular' approach whereby various toxins or drugs which are foreign to the body are prescribed in the hope that they will help the illness being treated. These drugs may indeed help to alleviate the symptoms, but they always create other unwanted side effects or iatrogenic (drug-induced) illnesses.

Personally, I do not believe that the use of tranquillisers to alleviate phobic anxiety is the answer.

One problem with these drugs is the side effects, the most common being: drowsiness, poor coordination, unsteadiness, blurred vision (this is more common when coming off tranquillisers than when taking them regularly), and uncharacteristic aggression.

There are certain benefits to using tranquillisers *occasionally*, after careful thought. If for example, there is no other way of controlling your phobic anxiety in a given situation, such as when flying, then tranquillisers prescribed by a doctor can be quite helpful to calm and sedate you.

However, if your anxiety is not so incapacitating, then I would strongly recommend taking natural remedies which will calm and alleviate the tension, without any unpleasant side effects. As these nutrients are natural substances found in food, by definition they do not need a prescription from a doctor. The secret is knowing which nutrients to take and in what combination, as their optimum effect occurs when they work synergistically, or as a team. Most of these natural remedies are freely available in chemists and health food shops.

Diet and Anxiety

The type of food you eat can either increase or decrease your anxiety. Some of the major stimulants, for example alcohol, coffee, chocolate, cola and cigarettes can exacerbate our anxiety levels. For example, alcohol can inhibit the mobilisation of reserve glucose from the liver and depress the demand for more sugar by a part of the brain called the hypothalamus, thus contributing to low blood sugar problems. Coffee contains theobromine, theophylline and caffeine, all of which act as stimulants. Cocoa also contains theobromine, and cola drinks contain caffeine too. These also have a tendency to stimulate the pancreas which releases insulin, which again will reduce blood sugar levels.

Let us briefly look at the right type of foods to eat on board, and those that are best avoided. In times of fear and anxiety it is always best to eat light, raw, fresh foods such as vegetables, fruit, nuts and seeds. Crunch on as much of them as you like, they are truly good for you.

Avoid the following acid-producing foods such as meat, fish and cheeses. It would also be wise to give a miss to all stimulants such as coffee, tea and alcohol. These tend to exacerbate the anxiety and stress reaction. Tea, coffee and other caffeine-containing drinks such as cola and Lucozade can actually mimic some of the symptoms of anxiety, therefore setting up a vicious cycle.

I suggest that you eat a light lunch or dinner on the aeroplane, and drink plenty of water. When you make your booking, request a vegetarian meal. This costs no extra, and will probably contain salad and fruit, excellent foods for our purposes. (Remember, it is too late to ask for a special meal when you arrive at the airport.) Camomile tea is a natural relaxant, so take some sachets with you (the cabin crew will provide the hot water) and drink 3–4 cups of this throughout the flight.

It is best not to add sugar, as white sugar (sucrose) stimulates your pancreas to secrete insulin, which reduces your blood sugar levels rapidly. This may lead to low blood sugar which again mimics a lot of symptoms very similar to anxiety and tension. When the blood sugar level drops we may feel confused, forgetful, have difficulty concentrating, be impatient and irritable, and develop headaches and emotional instability. These are all symptoms of the anxiety that we are trying to alleviate.

If we constantly eat sugar, the pancreas is continuously stimulated. The pancreas produces insulin which helps to take the sugar out of the blood and store it in the liver. If we eat any carbohydrate in refined form (white sugar, sweets, chocolate, white flour and its products, as well as stimulants such as caffeine and nicotine) digestion is rapid, and glucose enters the blood in a violent rush. In each case, the pancreas can overreact and produce too much insulin. This will lead to the blood sugar taking a very rapid nose-dive, and dropping too low for normal functioning.

This worsens your existing anxiety and fear. All the other stimulants mentioned above, as well as sugar and any sweet foods can trigger a rapid drop in your blood sugar levels and so should be avoided, at least throughout the course of the flight. Remember that fruit juices contain sugar that is rapidly converted to glucose by the body. Try diluting juices with mineral water, or soda water. Try to eat small, frequent meals, preferably containing protein or complex carbohydrates such as fruit, whole-wheat bread, pulses, nuts, vegetables and fish and meat.

The Natural Tranquillisers

Scientists have discovered that when we are anxious and stressed, our brain waves tend to speed up from their usual slow, relaxed alpha waves, to faster, more alert beta waves. There are many ways of slowing down these brain waves and therefore rebalancing the stress response.

Most people do this by taking prescription tranquillisers. As we have already seen, these will inevitably have some type of unwanted side effects. What most people want to do when they are stressed and anxious is to relax, but at the same time be clear-headed, alert and focused.

Over the last two or three decades, nutritionists and orthomolecular specialists have found *natural* substances that help alleviate anxiety. These occur naturally in food and include nutrients such as amino acids, vitamins, minerals, metals and trace elements.

The simplest way to take in many of these nutrients is to take a good multivitamin/multimineral formula. Take these tablets as prescribed on the pack. As a rough guide, a good multivitamin/mineral formula will contain at least 30–50mg B-complex vitamins, so look for this on the pack. If in doubt about any of these nutritional supplements, you can always ask your local nutritionist for further information.*

The effect of these nutrients is not going to be a sudden relaxation, as one would expect from a powerful tranquilliser. Instead, it will take a little while before you begin to feel the soothing effects – maybe half an hour or so, so you need to take these at least 30–60 minutes before the flight.

Please note that the authors cannot accept responsibility for anyone taking these remedies without the guidance of a qualified practitioner – these are only guidelines which the person reading will take ultimate responsibility for.

Herbal Formulas

In addition to these nutritional supplements you could also take a good herbal formula, again readily available in tablet form from leading chemists and health food shops.

One is called Natracalm and contains a plant extract called *Passiflora incarnata*, commonly known as the passion flower. The other is Valerina which contains valerian extract, hops extract, *Humulus lupules*, lemon balm extract and melissa extract, all herbs scientifically known to have a sedative and tranquillising effect, without any side effects. I suggest that you begin taking these a few days, or even a couple of weeks before you trip, in order to give your body some time to adjust to a new relaxed mode.

Generally, it is OK to take these herbs, but if in doubt, ask a qualified medical herbalist. Women who are pregnant or breast-feeding should not take these herbs, or any others without prior expert advice. If you are on any type of drugs, DO NOT try to stop these by yourself without first consulting your prescribing doctor.

Bach Flower Remedies

I believe that everyone should read one of Dr Bach's books – he was truly an amazing physician, pathologist, immunologist, bacteriologist, homeopath and researcher, but above all, he was an incredibly altruistic person. I use his remedies every day in my clinical practice with absolutely amazing results. I use them instead of tranquillisers and psychotropic (brain-changing) drugs.

A few of the remedies that I feel will be helpful in cases of fear, anxiety and panic are listed below. Again, these are freely available in most chemists and health food stores.

Rock Rose – for extreme terror, panic, hysteria, fright and nightmares.

Mimulus – for known fears, for example, flying, fear of heights, pain, darkness, death, etc. Also for timidity and shyness.

Cherry Plum – for fear of losing mental and physical control; uncontrolled, irrational thoughts.

Aspen – for vague fears and anxieties of unknown origin, a sense of foreboding, apprehension, or impending disaster.

White Chestnut – Persistent, unwanted thoughts. Preoccupation with some worry or episode. Mental arguments.

Impatiens – impatience and irritability.

I suggest that you buy all 6 of these remedies, buy a

30ml amber medicine bottle with dropper, fill this with mineral water, and then place 2 drops of each remedy into the bottle. Shake it up, and take 4 drops, 4 times daily. Begin this a few weeks before your trip, and I am certain that all will go well.

There is one final remedy which is an absolute must!

Rescue Remedy
Rescue Remedy was named by Dr Bach for its calming and stabilising effect on the emotions during a crisis. This is why it is ideally suited for flying fears, and is included as part of this book. It is ideally suited for any imbalance in the psychological or emotional state of a person, as often occurs during an anxiety or panic attack.

Rescue Remedy can be used in combination with the other remedies already mentioned. Rescue Remedy has been shown to be non-toxic, non-habit-forming, and free from side effects. However, it should be noted that Rescue Remedy is *not* meant to be a panacea or a substitute for emergency medical treatment.

You may buy the Rescue Remedy in a liquid concentrate form. Place four drops of this concentrate into a quarter glass of liquid. Sip every 3–5 minutes or more often as necessary. Hold in mouth a moment before swallowing.

If water or other beverages are not available, then Rescue Remedy may be taken directly from the concentrate bottle by placing 4 drops under the tongue. Drops may also be added to a spoonful of water if desired.

For those unable to drink, the remedy may be rubbed directly from the concentrate bottle on the lips, behind the ears, or on the wrists. The Rescue Remedy is also available in cream form, which again can be rubbed on the skin, where it will be directly absorbed.

There is absolutely no reason why you should not be able to lie back and enjoy a quiet, peaceful trip, free from anxiety, fear and tension. These symptoms are not all in the mind; they are true physiological reactions of the body that can now be controlled using a nutritional and natural approach. Should you want to find out more about your health from a natural and nutritional perspective then I suggest that you visit a qualified nutritionist, herbalist, naturopath or natural therapist at the next available opportunity. These therapists will be able to assess your existing health and develop a programme that will help to optimise your health.

CONQUER YOUR FEAR OF FLYING

The natural therapies that I have mentioned are by no means conclusive. There are many other types of therapies that could be but I have tried to be as practical as possible in giving suggestions that can be implemented while actually on the flight.

I sincerely hope that this little section on how to decrease your anxiety has worked for you, and that you may even have enjoyed your flight. If your anxiety level was still high, perhaps it would be a good to visit a natural therapist of the kind mentioned above. They should be able to help you cure both your phobia and your anxiety once and for all!

For those that have benefited from the book, I would love to hear from you at the following address:

Dr George J. Georgiou, Ph.D.
Natural Therapy Centre
P.O. Box 2008
6530 Larnaca
Cyprus
Tel: ++ 357 99 682083
Fax: ++ 357 24 624434

Good luck, happy flying, and God bless!

Appendix 1

Dr Yaffé's 10 Golden Rules for Taking the Fear out of Flying

These were formulated by the late Dr Maurice Yaffé, the psychological director of the Air Travel Anxiety Seminar. Dr Yaffé's excellent book is called *Taking the Fear out of Flying*.

1. When flying is viewed as a threat, panicky feelings are often the result. Don't worry: these are normal – albeit exaggerated – reactions. Avoidance or escape only keep the problem going; they do not help resolve it.

2. Nothing worse can happen to you. All that follows anxiety is relaxation.

3. Focus on the here-and-now, and what is actually happening. The future will take care of itself.

4. Monitor your breathing and make sure your pattern is slow and relatively deep – as opposed to fast and shallow. Don't hold your breath.

5. Adopt the view that everything is normal unless you are told absolutely and incontrovertibly otherwise by those who know, i.e. the professional flight crew.

6. Give yourself permission to be here. Adopt the view that you have nothing better to do than go through with the experience. Remember the reasons that made you decide to confront the situation in the first place.

7. Feelings follow behaviour rather than the reverse: you have to attend to what happens on a flight to feel better about it. So, for example, look out of the cabin window in order to become comfortable about it. Don't wait to feel in the mood to do so.

8. Take positive action. Start to relax as soon as you feel any signs of tension or anxiety, or if for any reason the level increases.

9. Don't jump to conclusions. What is the hard evidence on which you are basing your negative views? Are there alternative explanations for what you are thinking?

10. At the end of the trip, note down how it really was –

NOT what you think it should have been like. Highlight what helped, and what you need to attend to next time. On your next flight, take a brief list of 'personal statements'. Learning to feel comfortable about flying is a skill like any other, and so practice is necessary to get it completely right. Taking another flight within a few weeks is likely to speed up the process.

Appendix 2

Still Uneasy About Flying?

Courses

If you would like to learn more, or still feel apprehensive about flying, Aviatours Ltd, together with British Airways, run special courses that are designed to reassure you and make your next flight more relaxing and enjoyable.

These one-day courses include a short flight and are run by highly experienced British Airways pilots and a trained psychologist. They are available at London Heathrow, Birmingham, Manchester, and Glasgow and the cost (2002 prices) varies between about £180 and £215, depending on the location. There is usually a course running at one of these locations once a month. For details, contact Aviatours at the address below.

Aviatours also supply a small book, *Are You Afraid to Fly?* which costs £6.00 including post and packing; a relaxation audio tape, at £7.50 including p&p; and a video, *Are You Afraid To Fly?*, at £15.50 including p&p.

CONQUER YOUR FEAR OF FLYING

To find out more, or order these products, please contact: Aviatours Ltd., 'Pinewoods', Eglinton Road, Rushmoor, Surrey GU10 2DH. Tel: 01252-793250

Britannia Airways run courses twice yearly at East Midlands Airport, similar to the Aviatours course mentioned above. These courses cost (in 2002) £150 for the full course, including a one hour fifteen minute flight, a copy of a book *Flying with Confidence*, and a video of aircraft sights and sounds. The flight alone costs £50. Contact: The Passenger Relations Department, Britannia Airways Ltd, Luton Airport, Beds, LU2 9ND. Tel: 01582 424155.

Individual therapy
Emily Jacob, who also works with Aviatours, runs individual therapy sessions in London. Tel: 0208-878-5835

Books and Tapes
1. *Plane Scared* is a useful, eleven-page booklet produced to accompany Channel 4's documentary of the same name. To order a copy, send £1 (cheques made payable to Channel 4 Television) to Plane Scared, P.O. Box 4000, London W3 6XJ.

FLYING? NO FEAR!

2. *Fly without Fear* is a tape produced by Lifeskills Ltd, who also offer individual counselling. The tapes cost £8.50 + £1.00 post and packing. Contact: Lifeskills Ltd., Bowman House, 6 Billetsfield, Taunton TA1 3NN

4. *Taking the Fear out of Flying* Dr Maurice Yaffé's book, published by David and Charles. Available from booksellers, or by mail order for £8.50, including post & packaging, from Aviatours (see address above).

5. A video, *Are you Afraid to Fly?* costing £15.50, and a booklet of the same title, costing £6, (both including post and packaging), are available from Aviatours (see address above).

Medicament

The writer is not qualified to comment on the advisability or suitability of tranquillisers, etc, but a homeopathic practitioner advised him that the homeopathic remedy Aconite is effective. One 200c tablet should be taken on the morning of a flight, and another just before the trip starts.

Bibliography

Erdmann, R. & Jones, M. *The Amino Revolution: The most exciting development in nutrition since the vitamin tablet* (1989, Century Hutchinson Ltd)

Hanson, P. *The Joy of Stress* (1988, Pan Books)

Holford, P. *Optimum Nutrition Workbook: All the Facts You Need to Know for a Healthy Life* (1992, ION Press)

Looker, T. & Gregson, O. *Stresswise: A Practical Guide for Dealing with Stress* (1989, Hodder and Stoughton Educational)

Murray, M. & Pizzorno, J. *Encyclopaedia of Natural Medicine* (1992, Macdonald Optima)

Ody, P. *The Herb Society's Complete Medicinal Herbal* (1993, Dorling Kindersley)

Ramsell, J. *Questions and Answers: The Bach Flower Remedies* (1991, The C.W. Daniel Company Limited)

FLYING? NO FEAR!

Trattler, R. *Better Health Through Natural Healing* (1985, Thorsons)

Vlamis, G. *Rescue Remedy: The Healing Power of Bach Flower Rescue Remedy* (1994, Thorsons)

Yaffé, M. *Taking the Fear out of Flying* (1990, David & Charles)